Land Stewardship in
The Next Era of Conservation

by
V. Alaric Sample

for the
Pinchot Institute for Conservation
Grey Towers National Historic Landmark
Milford, Pennsylvania

Copyright © 1991 by the Pinchot Institute for Conservation

Introduction by James W. Giltmier and Sara Ebenreck

All rights reserved. No portion of this book may be reproduced by any process or technique without the express consent of the publisher.

ISBN: 0-938549-04-9

Designed and printed by the Society of American Foresters

Photographs reprinted by permission of the USDA Forest Service

Published by Grey Towers Press, P.O. Box 188, Milford, PA 18337

Manufactured in the United States of America

Contents

"Hurt not the earth, neither the sea, nor the trees."
—Revelation 7:3

Foreword:

The Evolution of the Grey Towers Protocol

by James W. Giltmier
and
Sara Ebenreck

THIS PUBLICATION GREW OUT OF A CONFERENCE on land stewardship that was part of the celebration of the 1991 Centennial of the National Forests. Birthdays and anniversaries are important milestones in the development of people and institutions. They provide us with an opportunity to look backward at the path we have followed. But more importantly they provide a stopping place to look out to the horizon to glimpse a shadow of the future. Most of all, these occasions give us the chance to adjust our course headings, if that seems appropriate.

We began this look forward on November 5th and 6th of 1990. Under the auspices of the Centennial of the National Forests, the Pinchot Institute for Conservation brought approximately 30 people together at Grey Towers, the family home of Gifford Pinchot. They were of many different occupations and points of view. Some cared about the land as a producer of commodities, while others worried that the term "land management" inherently meant despoiling nature. Philosophers and writers, foresters and farm advocates, scientists and lobbyists, engineers and college professors, all convened at the two-day seminar, brought together by a common thread: a deep caring for the land.

Our purpose was presumptuous and exciting. We wanted to look over the edge, into the distance to see if we could come up with some common ideals about future stewardship of the land—to arrive at some over-arching principles for land stewardship in the years to come.

The criteria for these principles was that if they were followed, they would—based on the science we now know and our best instincts as lovers of the land—provide us with a sustainable existence on the Earth. More than just providing us with enough food, shelter, and other commodities needed for a world population that could well double in size, this stewardship must also respect the needs of the ecosystem itself, independent of its producing capacity.

What we tried to do at Grey Towers was to create a laboratory slide that was a cross section of knowledge about the social, scientific, economic, ethical, and political aspects of land stewardship, plus a small measure of the love, magic, and fire that each participant brings to the land.

Al Sample's paper speaks in great measure to scientific land management and the need for more research. And those are very important things. But having said them, we admit that there is much about natural systems that we do not know from science, nor can we deduce it from economics. "Love," "respect," and "sharing" were important words that the group at Grey Towers used often. And while scientific assessments and technical knowledge about ecosystems may guide particular actions about the land, the fact that humans care about the land—that they love it—is a fundamental basis for a steward-ship ethic. In order for professional natural resource managers to exert leader-ship in the care of natural systems, they must first demonstrate that they truly care for the resources they manage. As Aldo Leopold put it, "We can be ethical only in relation to something we can see, feel, understand, love, or otherwise have faith in."

Generations of foresters have testified that it is a love for the outdoors, for trees, wildlife, and all of the complex qualities of particular forests that is an essential part of what draws them into that profession. Similarly it is a deeply felt concern about the loss of special places such as old-growth forests, wild areas, or single ancient trees that motivates much public concern to protect them.

The love of nature is not abstract. It is a powerful force that pulls us to spend time with the places we love, to notice how they are doing, to learn the signs of their health and illness. It is worth noting that the well-quoted Leopold essay on "The Land Ethic" was part of a larger work, *The Sand County Almanac,* chronicling a year spent by the conservationist on his small patch of Wisconsin sand lands. In the almanac Leopold speaks of learning to "live by the land," not simply "on it." He tracked wildlife to learn how its territorial "beat" intersected with human ownership lines. And he spoke of the joy that came from cherishing those acres, as well as the grief that comes from damage to them. "We grieve," he wrote, "not for names in a botany book, but only for the loss of particular plants that we know."

It is such a love of the land that puts our stewardship ethic in the context of a larger relationship. As stewards, we have certain powers to manage the land. As lovers of the land, we know that we are relating to an enormous reality. The forest is an important part of the Earth, and it all is a part of the cosmos—something much larger than us—for which the proper response is a deep gratitude and joy, even humility and awe. At such moments, tough, pragmatic stewards everywhere share the thought of the great medieval mystic, Meister Eckhart, who said that the fundamental prayer needed in this life is a "thank you."

The Grey Towers Protocol

The group at Grey Towers was asked to arrive at a set of land stewardship principles that incorporated into it an ethical understanding—or more simply, the rules for "give and take" in a community; the knowledge that we not only get from the land, but that much must be given to it as well.

After an exciting and challenging two days, the group emerged with a set of four principles:

1. Management activities must be within the physical and biological capabilities of the land, based upon comprehensive, up-to-date resource information and a thorough scientific understanding of the ecosystem's functioning and response.

2. The intent of management, as well as monitoring and reporting, should be making progress toward desired future resource conditions, not on achieving specific near-term resource output targets.

3. Stewardship means passing the land and resources—including intact, functioning forest ecosystems—to the next generation in better condition than they were found.

4. Land stewardship must be more than good "scientific management"; it must be a moral imperative.

There is an important postscript to all of this, and it comes from a participant in our seminar who is not a land steward. He is Jim Nash, Executive

Director of the Center for Theology and Public Policy in Washington, D.C. If we were to ask Jim, he would add a fifth item that to him would be essential to a complete land stewardship protocol. For the pragmatists that additional item might be stated: "Know when to leave well enough alone."

Jim spoke of the need to respect the rights of plant and animal species as equals to humans, the need to save some land for wilderness, and to "use" only those lands that are needed. Because these ideas on land stewardship are for the readers of this publication to take or leave as they see fit, it is for you to decide whether Jim's number five belongs in your intellectual kit bag.

When the session was completed, no one felt that we had created a new set of moral imperatives for the management of land. But the group was sufficiently satisfied with its combined output to call it the "Grey Towers Protocol." It is not a prescription for how others should live and manage their land. It simply says, "This is what we think, and we would like to share our ideas with others."

As George Santayana wrote, "When Socrates and his two great disciples composed a system of rational ethics, they were hardly proposing practical legislation for mankind. . . . They were merely writing an eloquent epitaph for their country." There was an element of patriotism reflected by the participants as well; only it is not so much nationalism as caring for the home place.

The people who contributed to the Grey Towers Protocol do not presume that their work should be a national epitaph. But they do hope that this document will provide others with some of the ideas they might need to look off into the future of natural resource management, in other words, an appropriate look forward for the Centennial of the National Forests.

All of the participants are grateful to V. Alaric Sample of the American Forestry Association, who was the chronicler of the Grey Towers sessions, and for the hospitality of Ed Brannon, the Director of Grey Towers.

We are especially grateful to Rob Hendricks, the Director of the Centennial celebration who made it possible for this to be the first in a series of Grey Towers Press publications which we will call *Breaking New Ground*. We also thank the Publications Department of the Society of American Foresters and Nancy Pittman, editor of this publication.

James W. Giltmier is the Executive Vice President of the Pinchot Institute for Conservation. Sara Ebenreck is a philosopher and the editor of *Earth Ethics*.

Invited Panelists

Seminar on Land Stewardship
Grey Towers National Historic Landmark
Milford, Pennsylvania
November 5-6, 1990

1. Dr. William Klein, Director, Fairchild Tropical Garden

2. Roy Gray, Chief, Soil Conservation Service

3. William Banzhaf, Executive Vice President, Society of American Foresters

4. Douglas Wheeler, The Resources Agency, State of California

5. Jeff Sirmon, Deputy Chief, Programs & Legislation, USDA Forest Service

6. Charles Philpot, Director, Pacific Northwest Research Station, USDA Forest Service

7. Kevin Coyle, President, American Rivers

8. Rupert Cutler, Director, Lewis and Clark Environmental Center

9. Peter V. Jackson, Executive Vice President, Society for Range Management

10. Sara Ebenreck, Editor, *Earth Ethics,* Professor, St. Mary's College of Maryland

11. Hal Salwasser, Director, New Perspectives, USDA Forest Service

12. Rob Hendricks, Director, National Forest Centennial, USDA Forest Service

13. Ed Brannon, Director, Grey Towers

14. Neill Schaller, Associate Director, Institute for Alternative Agriculture

15. Al Sample, Senior Associate, American Forestry Association

16. Dennis Le Master, Chairman, Department of Forestry, Purdue University

17. Jackie Tuxill, New England environmentalist

18. Janice McDougle, Wildlife & Fisheries Staff, USDA Forest Service

19. Susan Odell, Recreation Management Staff, USDA Forest Service

20. Stephen P. Mealey, Supervisor, Boise National Forest, USDA Forest Service

21. Jim Nash, Center for Theology and Public Policy, Wesley Theological Seminary

22. Michael T. Rains, Director, NE Area Office, USDA Forest Service

23. Max Schnepf, Soil & Water Conservation Society

24. R. Neil Sampson, Executive Vice President, American Forestry Association

25. Daniel Schaeffer, "Forum for Applied Research & Applied Public Policy," University of Tennessee Energy, Environment & Resources Center

26. Kathy Kohm, Editor, "Forest Perspectives" bulletin

27. Robert A. Denman, Legislative Assistant, National Farmers Union

28. Dudley L. Willis, Physical Engineer

"The future of the biosphere is inseparable from the future of the human mind . . . the destiny of every species and every ecosystem depends on what kind of progress is made in the realm of human thought and action."
—WALTER TRUETT ANDERSON

Preface

SHORTCOMINGS IN NATURAL RESOURCE MANAGEMENT in the global environment as well as at home have caused many Americans to re-examine the concepts of natural resource conservation and stewardship that seemed to have served us well in the past. This is not the first time that such soul-searching has taken place. The Creative Act of 1891, which authorized the forest reserves that later became the basis for today's National Forest System, was one manifestation of a fundamental shift that took place in the attitudes and values of the American public to the nation's land and natural resources in the latter half of the nineteenth century. During the previous three centuries of European settlement, these social attitudes were defined by the need to conquer a wilderness continent and by the perception that resources such as timber and wildlife were so abundant in North America as to be practically inexhaustible. Many see the 1864 publication of George Perkins Marsh's *Man and Nature* as the beginning of a basic shift in the public attitude toward natural resources, from unfettered exploitation to one of conserving resources to provide a sustained yield of those commodities—primarily timber, range, and water—needed to sustain an expanding population. This attitude was also reflected in the shift from the rapid disposal of public lands into private ownership under such laws as the Homestead Act of 1862 to the reserving of public lands to meet the needs of broader society, under such laws as the Creative Act of 1891.

As we pause to celebrate the centennial of this momentous law, social attitudes and values are once again shifting to define what now appears will be the third major era in the history of Americans' relationship to their lands and natural resources. Perhaps stimulated by the extreme examples of depletion and degradation of forests in the tropics, we are now beginning to recognize forests as far more than just warehouses of goods maintained for human use and consumption. Perhaps more than any other single issue, the plight of endangered species has forced us to recognize that forest ecosystems—and the life forms that inhabit them—have values that transcend those of direct human utility. The concepts of sustained yield and multiple use, which have served us well over the past century, are gradually being rewritten in terms of sustainable ecosystem management. The focus is less on guaranteeing a continuous flow of products and more on maintaining or improving resource conditions so as not to leave forest ecosystems diminished from what they were when they came under our care.

The notion of stewardship—the care and fostering of something that is entrusted to someone on behalf of others—was at the heart of the nineteenth century conservation movement. It is fair to say that this concept, perhaps in simplified form, plays a large role in guiding the decisions and management actions of resource managers across the nation every day. Employees of the Forest Service clearly do not own the national forest lands they manage; but each strives to adhere to the goals and values of the common weal, as best they can interpret them. The concept of stewardship applies equally well to private lands. Many farmers view themselves as husbanding the productivity of their lands for the sake of those who will follow, whether their own children and grandchildren or others. They view the land as theirs to use, but also to pass along to future generations in good condition.

As we move from the era of sustained yield to the era of sustainable ecosystem management, we are challenged also to adapt the notion of stewardship that guides both long-term resource management planning and day-to-day decisionmaking. Do we really know what stewardship means? Is there common agreement on a few guiding principles or components of what constitutes stewardship? Would we recognize good stewardship if we saw it on the land? Is there a difference between defining stewardship and having the freedom and flexibility to practice it?

These are among the questions addressed by a group of distinguished individuals brought together under the auspices of the Pinchot Institute for Conservation at Grey Towers National Historic Landmark, the family home of Gifford Pinchot. These individuals—farmers and philosophers, foresters and theologians—have in one way or another devoted a great deal of thought to the values that define society's relationship with land and natural resources. They came together for two days in the Great Hall at Grey Towers to reflect on the ideals and accomplishments of some of the early leaders in conservation—Marsh, Pinchot, Muir, Leopold and others—and to explore the ways in which those ideals might evolve to meet the challenges of the second century after the passage of the Creative Act. The Great Hall was the scene of some of the lively discussions and impassioned debates that ushered in the first great era of conservation in America. The Pinchot Institute for Conservation is grateful for the time and effort invested by the seminar participants in helping to guide us all into what we hope will be the next great era of conservation.

V. ALARIC SAMPLE

Milford, Pennsylvania

July 1, 1991

"A man is ethical only when life, as such, is sacred to him, that of plants and animals as that of his fellow men, and when he devotes himself helpfully to all life that is in need of help."

—ALBERT SCHWEITZER

Introduction

THE CREATIVE ACT OF 1891 was a revolution in the philosophy and attitude of Americans to the nation's land and natural resources. Manifest Destiny fulfilled, the western frontier had been declared closed three decades earlier, prompting a few observers to recognize that the resources of North America were perhaps finite after all and that their unbridled exploitation, heedless of the needs of the future, could soon bring unprecedented hardships to a burgeoning young nation. As early as 1864, George Perkins Marsh observed that the indiscriminate lumbering of forests in the eastern United States had resulted in drought, floods, erosion, and unfavorable climatic changes.[1] Similar abuse of the land had been responsible, Marsh believed, for the deforestation and subsequent decline of the Mediterranean empires, in both ecological and economic terms.[2] He pleaded that we "be wise in time, and profit by the errors of our older brethren." Society's attitudes toward the land at that time were largely defined by the admonition in Genesis to "be fruitful and multiply, and fill the earth and subdue it; and have dominion over every living thing that moves upon the earth."[3] Marsh took a second look at this passage, and at God's placement of man in the Garden of Eden to "till it and keep it,"[4] and concluded that "man has too long forgotten that the earth was given to him for usufruct alone, not for consumption, still less for profligate waste."[5]

Marsh's perspective was quite utilitarian; it was not so much a question of environmental ethics as of protecting the earth's ability to support mankind.[6] The conservation movement of the late nineteenth century was concerned primarily with avoiding the depletion of the nation's forest resources by protecting the remaining forests from unnecessary waste, and from the devastating fires that often followed in the wake of the lumbering.[7] The nation's population was growing quickly, and new towns were springing up all over the West. During the decade 1865-1875, the mileage of railroads more than doubled, as did the value of lumber produced.[8] An 1865 report from the U.S. Commissioner of Agriculture predicted a "permanent national famine of wood" within thirty years.[9] The commissioner of the General Land Office in the Department of the Interior declared that "in forty or fifty years our own forests would have disappeared and those of Canada would be approaching exhaustion."[10] Clearly a key motivation of the nineteenth century conservation movement was a consuming fear that we would soon be depleted of one of the basic natural resources necessary to sustain the nation's economic growth and prosperity.

The evolution of conservation thought

It was this context—the need to manage the nation's forest resources for a sustained yield of renewable commodity resources such as timber and livestock forage—that would define conservation in America for much of the next century. The Creative Act of 1891, also known as the Forest Reserve Act,[11] represented an end to the period of exploitation and disposal of the public domain under such laws as the Homestead Act, the Timber and Stone Act, and the railroad land grants.[12] It authorized the President of the United States to reserve forest lands from the public domain, to be managed and protected for public purposes—and under public ownership—in perpetuity. This was a clear reversal from all U.S. public land policy up to that date, recognizing that there were important social values and services that could not be provided through the simple logic of private ownership and the responses of self-interested individuals to the forces of the economic market. This shift in philosophy was the impetus behind many of the social reforms of the period. The Creative Act of 1891 was one more manifestation of this shift in social values, and it marks the watershed between the era of exploitation and the era of conservation.

The Creative Act of 1891 provided a basis upon which subsequent federal laws refined the policies by which the forest reserves were to be managed as well as established. The Organic Act of 1897 called for the administration of the forest reserves "to improve and protect the forest . . . secure favorable conditions for water flows, and to furnish a continued supply of timber for the use and necessities of the citizens of the United States."[13] Despite some grumbling from commercial interests still promoting unregulated exploitation, most of the forest reserves established in the West between 1891 and 1897 were created upon petition from local citizens.[14] Having already suffered the effects of early forest exploitation, citizens in New Hampshire soon petitioned for what became the Weeks Law of 1911, extending the authority of the U.S. Forest Service to acquire lands in the East for addition to the National Forest System (including lands that are now part of New Hampshire's White Mountain National Forest).[15] The management of these reserves for a sustained yield of timber was seen as serving the broad public interest, both nationally and locally, for both forest products and a greater degree of economic stability.

A century later, sustained yield is a central tenet in the management of nearly all forest lands in the United States, public and private. The Creative Act of

1891, and the laws that subsequently reinforced and expanded upon its central purposes, have been successful in taking a fundamental shift in public values and attitudes and making it manifest on the land itself. But it was not achieved without significant turmoil and controversy, first in the three decades leading up to the passage of the Creative Act, and subsequently in the decades that followed, as this and related laws were implemented and enforced.

We are currently in the throes of another period of turmoil and controversy, borne of another fundamental shift in public philosophies and attitudes toward our land and natural resources. During the past three decades, forest resource managers have come under increasing criticism for failing to adapt what they do to reflect evolving public values. The wisdom of managing forest resources for a sustained yield has not changed. But the public now recognizes values in forests that subsume and transcend their value as storehouses for commodity resources. The value of forests for multiple uses, including non-commodity uses such as recreation and habitat for fish and wildlife, has been recognized in law, but it has also set the stage for a continuous and difficult balancing act for resource managers. More recently the unprecedented rate of loss of species in forest ecosystems has raised ethical issues and the question of whether we are sustaining timber yields while failing to sustain our forests as intact, functioning ecosystems.

The concept of stewardship was at the heart of the nineteenth century conservation movement. Marsh's notion that "the earth was given to man for usufruct," defined by Webster as "the right of using and enjoying the fruits or profits of something belonging to another," is one articulation of the broader idea of stewardship, itself defined by Webster as "the individual's responsibility to manage his life and property with proper regard to the rights of others." Like the concept of sustained yield, the nineteenth century perceptions of what constitutes good stewardship have served us well for many years. Nonetheless, they too must be re-examined in light of the social, economic, and cultural changes that have taken place.

"*Man masters nature not by force but by understanding.*"
—JACOB BRONOWSKI

Stewardship as a set of guiding principles for resource managers

WHAT CONSTITUTES GOOD STEWARDSHIP is important to more than just philosophers and academics. The perceptions that have served in years past, embodied in the principles of sustained yield and the protection of the long-term productivity of soil and water resources, comprise the mental framework used by resource managers for planning and evaluating nearly every operation that takes place on the land itself. It is the why that forms the logical basis for what they do out on the ground: how they design a timber sale, where they route a road in a sensitive drainage, what to do about a trail or campsite that is suffering from overuse. Society is telling resource managers that this mental framework is no longer valid, that a new perspective is needed. Among resource managers, years of resistance are gradually crumbling and giving way to simple confusion: if the old framework is growing obsolete, what is the new framework? It is difficult for resource managers to know what to do if they no longer have a clear idea of the driving forces behind why they are doing it. The confusion is interpreted as a failure of leadership, or even of competency, and public resentment grows.

Just what are the concepts of stewardship that should now guide the management of our forest resources? And how can they be inculcated so that they become as thoroughly incorporated in the value system of resource management professionals as sustained yield has been?

The group that gathered at Grey Towers to explore the emerging concepts of land stewardship perceived themselves as fellow travelers on a road whose destination is still unknown, recognizing that they could not expect to definitively articulate every aspect. Four guiding principles for good land stewardship emerged, although the list is neither comprehensive nor exhaustive.

1.   *Management activities must be within the physical and biological capabilities of the land, based upon comprehensive, up-to-date resource information and a thorough scientific understanding of the ecosystem's functioning and response.*

One of the first and most important elements in assuming any management task is a current, accurate inventory and understanding of the capability of the resources at hand. In many instances resource managers themselves are the first to recognize that the information available to them is inadequate to properly care for and efficiently manage the resources over which they have responsibility. Some of this is attributed to the short tenure that many resource managers have in any given location, particularly in the case of the national forests. This is compounded by the time they must devote to administrative work at the expense of getting out into the field. Between these two factors, resource managers hardly have a chance to gain a personal familiarity with the land itself and its resources and are not around long enough to observe personally the ecological results of their resource management decisions. A larger part of the problem, however, seems to be that many resource managing agencies and organizations are unable or unwilling to dedicate sufficient resources to updating inventories, validating growth and yield estimates, monitoring changes in resource conditions, and recognizing changes in patterns of public use. Resource users are often better apprised of such information than the managers; and where this becomes evident to users, it inevitably undermines their confidence in the ability of the manager to do his or her job effectively. The managers themselves often share this perception, adding to their frustration and diminishing their self-esteem as good land stewards.

In addition to shortcomings in data gathering, there is a fundamental lack of scientific understanding of the functioning of many forest ecosystems and their likely response to management activities. The National Research Council, a part of the National Academy of Sciences, recently assembled a committee of eminent natural scientists from universities and other research organizations around the country. In its report the committee described the current state of our knowledge regarding the functioning of forest ecosystems.

> Although concern about and interest in the global role and fate of forests are currently great, the existing level of knowledge about forests is inadequate to develop sound forest management policies. Current knowledge and patterns of research will not result in sufficiently accurate predictions of the consequences of potentially harmful influences on forests, including forest management practices that lack a sound basis in biological knowledge. This deficiency will reduce our ability to maintain or enhance forest productivity, recreation, and conservation as well as our ability to ameliorate or adapt to changes in the global environment.[16]

The committee called for a fundamental redefinition of forest science and the concepts that drive forest research at universities and other scientific institutions across the country. The central recommendation of the report was to broaden forestry research from the agricultural model of simply improving the production of commodities to one based upon gaining a better understanding of the functioning of healthy forest ecosystems, what the report termed an "environmental paradigm." This implicitly recognizes a key tenet of environmental ethics: that the vast array of biological and physical elements and the complex bonds of interdependency that link them in a healthy, functioning forest ecosystem have a value unto themselves, independent of their importance or utility for human purposes.

As inadequate as resource information might be for planning and management, the shortcomings in monitoring and evaluation are often even greater. Predictions made during resource planning cannot be adjusted to reflect the actual effects of management activities on the resources if those effects cannot be monitored and evaluated. Pronouncements that projects will not go forward unless they can be properly monitored ring hollow when many diverse pressures are brought on resource managers to carry out the provisions of their management plan. Thus errors made during the early stages of resource planning caused by inadequate or obsolete information are often not discovered and continue to be made, each iteration compounding the unintended impacts on the land and resources. This clearly is not a formula for good land stewardship.

Additional scientific research, both basic and applied, can reveal important new insights into both unanticipated needs and undreamed of opportunities.

From Rachel Carson's 1960 treatise on the environmental impacts of agricultural pesticides to recent space-based discoveries of holes in the Earth's ozone layer and the possible warming of our global atmosphere, new scientific information has been crucial to focusing our collective attention and motivating meaningful changes in our attitudes and behavior.

But research can also be used to delay timely action. Politicians routinely assign thorny policy controversies to special commissions and task forces in hopes that the issues won't surface again before the next election. Policymakers often interpret the lack of absolute certainty in scientific pronouncements as a reason for taking no action whatsoever, assuming that additional research will reduce that uncertainty—and also the political costs of taking remedial actions.

In order to stay within the biological and physical capabilities of the land, managers must first know what those capabilities are. Resource management decisionmaking must be based on sufficiently detailed and current information, and a thorough understanding of the resource base, interactions among the resources, and the multiple effects likely to result from a given set of management activities.

While additional research may be helpful, there is also the need to use existing scientific information more effectively. Policymaking and research analysis often run on different tracks. When the controversy over a resource issue becomes highly emotional, as has the debate over the fate of the remaining old-growth forests in the Pacific Northwest, facts seem to get in the way of political opponents intent on simply slugging it out.

Resource managers are often overwhelmed by the sheer volume of data they must assimilate. If it is not carefully targeted, additional research would simply add to this information overload. Researchers and analysts can aid resource managers by focusing their efforts on managers' information gaps, performing new research when needed but also helping managers to take full advantage of information that already exists—through research compilation, analysis, and synthesis. The separation between policymaking and research analysis may be as much an obstacle to improved forest ecosystem management as the lack of information.

2. *The intent of management, as well as monitoring and reporting, should be making progress toward desired future resource conditions, not on achieving specific near-term resource output targets.*

There is a strong tendency in forest resource management, usually reinforced by organizational systems of professional advancement and rewards, to focus on specific quantitative resource output targets rather than on how to move from current resource conditions to some set of desired future resource conditions. In the case of the national forests, a traditional focus on meeting timber sale targets has even engendered efforts to invent quantitative targets for resources such as wildlife and recreation; the hope is that establishing "hard" targets for programs such as recreation and wildlife will generate the same sort of support for these programs as it has for the timber program.

But for timber management, striving to meet resource output targets is fundamentally inconsistent with the principles of good land stewardship. If resource management is focused on the commitment to a particular schedule of timber volumes to be sold or harvested, then the resulting condition of the forest is necessarily a secondary and residual consideration—if it is considered at all. On the other hand, if the focus is on the condition of the forest twenty or fifty years hence, then alternatives for timing, location, and intensity of timber harvests can be explored within these parameters. For public agencies like the Forest Service, multi-resource planning may be easier if the various interests can focus on reaching agreement on desired future forest conditions rather than on near-term resource outputs, leaving it more to the resource managers to determine how the desired conditions are to be achieved.

When Navajo foresters reassumed the management of their tribal lands in Arizona from the Bureau of Indian Affairs, they attempted to apply traditional forest management and planning approaches, such as computerized optimization models based upon linear programming, to guide their decisionmaking. In linear programming, multiple forest management goals must be narrowed to a single objective, with the remaining objectives treated not as goals but as constraints upon achieving the single objective. What they found, however, is that such approaches are fundamentally inconsistent with the traditional native American philosophies regarding the relationship between mankind and the natural environment that nurtures it. Central to this philosophy is the notion that mankind might enjoy the benefits the earth yields up, but that they must be used in a way that does not leave the earth impaired either for its own sake or for the sake of its other inhabitants, human or otherwise.

The linear program planning approach was thus rejected and, finding no ready substitute, the Navajo Forestry Department set about developing a new planning and management model more consistent with tribal philosophies. In cooperation with scientists at Northern Arizona University, they are in the process of developing a planning system based on a somewhat different computer modeling technique known as goal programming. Goal programming allows a more flexible approach; multiple goals are treated as so many simultaneous objectives, all to be reached as closely as possible.[17] Development of this technique continues and may one day offer a key to applying steward-ship principles successfully even to highly complex multi-resource management in which the use of a computer-based analytical model is essential.

Among private forest landowners, a focus on desired future resource conditions may facilitate a better understanding by landowners of their own objectives for their forests. Many nonindustrial, private forest landowners, who collectively control nearly sixty percent of the commercial forest land in the United States, use their land primarily for recreation, providing wildlife habitat, or simply for aesthetic enjoyment. Others see their land as a potential source of income. Nearly all view their forests as a valuable asset to be used, but also to be cared for for future generations. However, the management approach that they are taking, which in many cases is no management at all, may not be leading to a realization of their vision. Substantial improvements are needed in education and technical assistance to landowners to help them achieve their stewardship objectives and, in so doing, help provide for society's needs for clean air and water, habitat for a diversity of plant and animal species, quality outdoor recreation experiences, and forest products—now and in the future.

Where public and private lands are intermixed, there are opportunities for cooperation in the pursuit of desired future resource conditions, especially in terms of stewardship of biological resources. Ecological boundaries seldom coincide with ownership boundaries, and natural ecological units should be managed with as much foresight and coherency as blocks of land under a single ownership. Being scrupulously careful at one end of a sensitive water-shed accomplishes little if another owner just downstream is oblivious to ecological or environmental considerations. At the same time, there should be a recognition of the comparative advantages of lands under different ownerships; institutionally some public forest lands may be better suited for a particular style of management than private forest lands in the same general area. Working cooperatively, each owner can capitalize on the distinctiveness of his or her own resources and opportunities to manage the overall ecological unit to achieve the desired future resource conditions.

3. *Stewardship means passing the land and resources—including intact, functioning forest ecosystems—to the next generation in better condition than they were found.*

Nurturing an asset so as to pass it along to the next generation in as good or better condition than it was received is central to the concept of stewardship, whether of the family farm or a trust account managed by the local bank. Where it involves forest resources, however, the term stewardship has taken on a deeper meaning. Just as the ideal of sustained yield management has evolved to the broader ideal of sustainable ecosystem management, stewardship has evolved from maintaining productivity and output potential to maximizing current use while maintaining the full array of options for management decisions for the next generation. Our current understanding of the complex interactions that take place within forest ecosystems is far from complete. Earth slides, silted salmon runs, and simplified ecosystems that are far below their expected productivity are mute witness that our science was not as conclusive as we thought it was and that perhaps some degree of technological humility is in order. Our science has improved, but we also recognize that we will probably understand these ecosystems a good deal more in two decades than we do now. Disposing of industrial wastes in Love Canal probably seemed like a fine idea at the time. Stewardship entails taking a conservative approach to manipulating forest ecosystems in order to avoid inadvertent, but perhaps substantial, damages to their functioning.

Maintaining options for the future requires that the existing biological richness and integrity of the ecosystem remain undiminished. In the traditional machismo that seems to persist in forestry, this is still regarded by many as a soft-hearted, "fuzzy," or liberal altruistic value. It is not. It is as hard-headed and utilitarian as a growth and yield table. Imagine what would have happened if, in our quest to simplify natural forests to favor a few commercial species, we had eliminated soil mycorrhiza. Their critical function in forest tree growth was discovered in tree nurseries where they had been eliminated through soil fumigation. Until its role as a nitrogen fixer was fully appreciated, red alder was hardly permitted to survive in intensively managed conifer stands.

This is not to say that a species must be shown to have current or potential economic value in order to justify its continued existence. Of the hundreds of thousands of plant or animal species in the world, it is doubtful that even five percent of the total could be put to economic use. Yet this diversity of species is critical to the integrity and stability of the ecosystems they comprise. As Aldo Leopold pointed out, "one basic weakness in a conservation system based wholly on economic motives is that most members of the land community have no economic value."[18] When efforts have been mounted to preserve threatened species, the arguments have had to be couched in economic terms. Leopold saw this as a subterfuge, a substitute for a land ethic.

> A system of conservation based solely on economic self-interest is hopelessly lopsided. It tends to ignore, and thus eventually to eliminate, many elements in the land community that lack commercial value, but that are as far as we know essential to its healthy functioning. It assumes . . . that the economic parts of the biotic clock will function without the uneconomic parts.[19]

A recent essay in *Time* noted that "Noah's directive was to preserve all species. Modern man has no such option. Some species are already doomed and . . . loss of habitat is pushing at least 20,000 species a year into extinction."[20] How much richer or more resilient to today's environmental stresses would our forest ecosystems be had we not lost the thousands of species that have already succumbed to the advance of humanity? We will never know. And we don't have the option to bring them back even if we did know. The history of human civilization is one of continuous expansion of our understanding and appreciation for the complexities and intricacies of the natural world. The fact that we do not currently understand the function or value of some particular component is no indication that it can be eliminated from the system without consequence. We can—and must—do better by our descendants than our forebears have done by us.

4. Land stewardship must be more than good "scientific management"; it must be a moral imperative.

Stewardship is a set of practices that grow out of an ethical commitment. The concepts of stewardship at the time of the passage of the Creative Act of 1891 reflected the revolution in ethical development taking place in this period of social reform. But our social and environmental ethics have continued to evolve over the past century, and the practice of stewardship must likewise evolve to continue to reflect these emerging values accurately.

In order for these broader social and environmental values to be reflected on the land, the ethical considerations that underlie the concept of stewardship must play a substantive role in the day-to-day decisionmaking of resource managers. For years resource managers have tried to deny that ethics have a role in land use planning and decisionmaking. Rational-comprehensive planning and million-dollar computer models were expected to give us the answers, unsullied by value judgments on the part of the decisionmaker. A former forest supervisor, whose experience with national forest planning was particularly arduous, has observed that "the problem with the planning process is that it is godless." Citizens involved in national forest planning here and elsewhere across the country have looked to the Forest Service for "leadership" and not found it. What both the forest supervisor and the citizens involved in forest planning seek is a set of core values to serve as a touchstone—a constant and reliable reference point by which to determine whether or not they are still on course.

Human civilization has been exploring social ethics, both secular and ecclesiastical, for several millennia; the extension of ethics to other species and to the land itself has been articulated by Leopold and others for at least half a century now.[21] But it is difficult for resource users and managers to grasp the relevance of these lofty concepts to their day-to-day decisionmaking. Perhaps more than any other single issue, the question of maintaining biological diversity has begun to change all that. As hard as economists have tried to quantify, evaluate, and otherwise mold the issue of how to maintain habitat for endangered species into one of how best to maximize present net value, the resource manager is still confronted with a stark and uncompromising choice: is it right to knowingly jeopardize the survival of another species in order to secure certain benefits for humankind?

What is meant by the term "moral imperative"? "Moral" is defined as "conforming to a standard of right behavior, operative on one's conscience or ethical judgment." In a diverse and fast-moving society, how much can we rely on the sharing of common values and a consistent influence of conscience? Most of the widely held values in society are codified in law, even the most basic. It is our own internal codes of moral conduct, not the law, that prevents most of us from committing murder. But there are individuals in society who apparently do not ascribe to that moral code. Not content to trust in the power of conscience alone, the oldest human societies of which we have found record have set out their "standards of right behavior" in terms of *law*, both to standardize expectations of one another's behavior and to justify sanctions against individuals who deviated from those expectations. For the righteous citizen, one's moral code carries its own imperative; but the law is there to keep all those other characters in line, too.

Law and policy have changed over the years to reflect a widening circle of entities with rights to moral and ethical treatment. As Aldo Leopold points out in the "Conservation Ethic" section of *A Sand County Almanac,* Ulysses was a righteous, law-abiding citizen when he returned home and hanged his misbehaving slave girls all on the same rope.[22] This was not murder. The circle of ethical treatment included the citizens of Athens but did not yet extend to slave girls. A series of landmark laws, laws that quite literally define the advance of human civilization, have continued to expand that circle—the Magna Carta, Declaration of Independence, Emancipation Proclamation, Nineteenth Amendment, Indian Citizenship Act, and Civil Rights Act each extended the right to ethical treatment to individuals who had previously had no such rights.[23] Only recently have scholars begun to recognize the Endangered Species Act as perhaps another momentous advance in the history of human civilization— the first measure to legally protect the rights of species other than humans to survive, with sanctions for anyone who deviated from this standard.

None of these ethical milestones was achieved without controversy and strife. Much of this came during the early implementation of these laws when formerly dominant interests recognized that extending new rights often meant new limitations on their own behavior or activities. And in nearly every case, there were new economic costs to be borne as well. These costs were resisted, but eventually they were absorbed and became part of the accepted fabric of a morally advancing society. Few now would advocate a return to slavery or child labor in order to bring back the low labor costs that once were considered indispensable to the nation's economic prosperity.

Renewable resource management in this country is going through its greatest period of change since the conservation movement of the turn of the century. Resource managers as well as policymakers are searching for new concepts to provide the context for their actions and decisions. The idea of a land ethic has been around for decades, but it has not been integrated into day-to-day, on-the-ground resource decisions. Managers in the field are evincing a receptivity to new concepts. They are expressing a need for a set of core values to help managers distinguish right from wrong.

Perhaps Leopold was just fifty years ahead of his time when he called upon resource managers to ". . . quit thinking about decent land use as solely an economic problem. Examine each question in terms of what is ethically and aesthetically right, as well as what is economically expedient. A thing is right when it tends to preserve the integrity, stability, and beauty of the biotic community. It is wrong when it tends otherwise."[24]

Striving to maintain the integrity, stability, and beauty of the ecosystems we are managing will inevitably mean working within limits that we did not consider years ago. But managing forests for sustained yield meant working within limits that were unimaginable when the frontier was expanding and the nation's resources seemed limitless. This restriction seemed economically costly at the time, but who among us is not grateful that our forebears chose to impose these near-term costs upon themselves so that this and future generations might benefit? Our generation was the first to see the limitations of our world from the viewpoint of Apollo IX. Our generation was the first to truly recognize and accept that it is fully within the capacity of the human species to virtually end all life on Earth. But our generation may also be the first to recognize that species and ecosystems of no immediate utility to man also have a moral right to survival—and that therein may lie the key to the future of humanity as well.

"We are locked into a system of 'fouling our own nest' so long as we behave only as independent, rational free-enterprisers."
—GARRET HARDIN

Creating the environment necessary for land stewardship principles to be successfully applied

CONTRARY TO POPULAR PERCEPTIONS, leadership is seldom exercised through the issuance of commands, particularly in democratic societies. Most often the power of even the heads of state of the world's greatest nations is essentially the power to persuade. Without the support and willing cooperation of the governed, a leader cannot lead.

Good land stewardship cannot be accomplished through legislative or executive fiat. Resource managers, and the public on whose behalf the resource managers are acting, must first believe that good land stewardship is in their best interest and is therefore worthy not only of their support, but also an acceptance of certain limits on their previous freedom of action.

Economic well-being as a condition for stewardship

We cannot expect long-term dedication to land stewardship without the involvement and commitment of the local population or until that population's basic human needs are met. Gifford Pinchot clearly recognized this in his emphasis on local decisionmaking and the management of national forests to meet local needs within the broad guidelines of a few national objectives. He recognized that the national forests could not survive as guarded preserves, especially where they held vital resources that were not adequately available from other sources. Use was permitted, subject to a few key principles, and that use engendered local support for the national forests and eventually for the principles upon which they were founded. Had local needs been ignored and the gates to the national forests barred, the forests would have been overrun, and the opportunity to establish the basic concepts of stewardship would have been wiped out along with most of the resources. Proving to the local population that support for conservation is in their self-interest is key to being able to practice good land stewardship, whether to save rainforests in Costa Rica, elephant habitat in Zaire, or old-growth forest ecosystems in Oregon.

Good land stewardship includes the realization that communities will need help in adjusting, both economically and socially, to the shift from sustained yield to sustainable ecosystem management. Limitations on historic levels of commodity production associated with better land stewardship may have broad societal benefits, but near-term costs are often far more concentrated geographically. Thus the evolution in society's values and attitudes must be matched by a willingness to share in the costs as well as the benefits of shifting to sustainable ecosystem management.

As land stewards, resource managers also must recognize that resource demands are not static but will continue to grow with an increasing population. Research and development of new technology can help serve more needs with fewer resources. Emerging technology for de-inking and recycling waste-paper may reduce the demand for roundwood for papermaking in the United States by nearly half by 1995, using 30 to 50 percent less energy and reducing air pollution by as much as 95 percent.[25] Improving the efficiency of resource use is no less a part of the stewardship responsibility than taking care of the land directly.

Empowering resource managers to carry out stewardship principles

Defining the principles of stewardship and incorporating them into the value system of resource managers is only a partial solution to getting the principles applied on the land. Managers must feel they have the support of their organization, their profession, and the public in making the tough choices that will inevitably arise.

Resource management policymaking today takes place in a highly fragmented political environment that makes any change from the status quo time-consuming, expensive, and sometimes nearly impossible. Whatever direction away from current policy might be contemplated, there always seems to be one of a myriad of special interests ready to assert its "veto power" and block any change that is perceived to be against its interest—even if the change is in the interest of nearly everyone else. The majority of interests sit silent on the sidelines because the proposed change neither hurts them nor significantly helps them directly. The result is policy that cannot move off dead-center, that is frozen in place. In this state of paralysis, policies cannot evolve to reflect changing social attitudes and values. Special interests then further promote their causes by criticizing policymakers as unresponsive.

Although it is unlikely that this situation will change appreciably in the near future, there are ways to recognize the obstacles and work around them. One technique that is used regularly is to create a crisis, real or only in the minds of the legislators, that forces them to act rather than risk some alternative outcome that could threaten them politically. However, understanding what it is that works about this technique may help in the discovery of other less cynical or manipulative techniques. The same special interests are there to block any measure that threatens them, but the sense of crisis motivates the array of other interests to support the measure actively instead of sitting on the sidelines. If a sufficiently large coalition of these other interests can be formed in favor of the measure, then even the highly vocal resistance of a single interest can often be overcome.

Stewardship is a powerful organizing theme with broad appeal. It can enable agencies and other institutions to articulate and develop broader public support for policies and programs consistent with its principles. But first, interest groups and the public at large must see that stewardship principles are in their interest.

Changes are also needed internally in resource management organizations and even within the forestry profession itself in order to empower managers to act confidently upon their principles. Congress has shown that it can reflect changing social attitudes. The Forest Service is demonstrating in many dramatic ways that it can adapt as well. In any large organization, however, it is among the middle level managers that change is most difficult to achieve, and without them it is difficult for the organization overall to accomplish significant change.[26] Changes taking place at the top can be slowed and diluted, and changes taking place at the bottom can be blocked, if middle management is not "on board." The most basic requirement for meaningful change to begin taking place on the ground is for middle managers to feel confident that the organization will stand fully behind good stewardship decisions that may be politically unpopular, whether locally or nationally.

At the same time, the organization's incentive and reward system may need to be reoriented to encourage good stewardship. Success must be defined differently. Recognition and advancement must be based not upon resource outputs or other short-term measures, but upon progress made toward long-term goals, articulated in terms of desired future resources conditions. Attainment of assigned resource output goals has long been the primary measure of performance for National Forest System line officers, from the district rangers to the chief. Like so many other modes of behavior that become deeply ingrained in organizational culture, managing to meet targets has sometimes become a millstone around the neck of innovation. Once the Forest Service is certain of its identity and objectives, it should reward on the basis of achieving those objectives, not on the basis of a system that has kept it embroiled in controversy.

Resource management professionals need to be strengthened by a uniform adherence to a code of ethics that incorporates stewardship principles. This code would transcend organizational policies of employers, public or private, and give them an independent basis upon which to act on their convictions. The medical profession's code of ethics, developed and administered through the American Medical Association, occasionally comes into conflict with hospital corporations. Medical professionals insistent upon adhering to ethical standards are strengthened by the knowledge that an employer cannot simply do without them or replace one professional with another more willing to ignore those ethical standards. Employers eventually recognize that to obtain the services of professionals, their policies must be consistent with the code of ethics, including those relating to good land stewardship.

Both resource managers and the public must come to a new understanding of leadership. It has long been clear that resource managers cannot regard themselves as barons ruling over their jurisdictions without regard to public opinion. On the other hand, forest managers are trained professionals with an understanding of forest environments borne of years of academic and professional experience. They have much to offer the public as stewards of their land and resources. Resource managers must reconcile their responsibility to take the initiative as leaders with their responsibility to be responsive to continually evolving public values. Further, these professionals must share what they know in order to shape responsible public values. Public participation in resource management decisionmaking must not be viewed as a derogation of professional managers' power or authority, but as an opportunity to build the public commitment that is necessary to manage effectively and achieve long-term goals and objectives. The public wants to be able to look to professional resource managers for leadership. They want initiatives that are based on a thorough scientific understanding of resource capabilities and ecosystem functions. And they want to be able to trust managers to make decisions that are consistent with a few ethically based core values that they see as carrying out the profession's responsibility for long-term stewardship of the nation's natural resources.

"We abuse the land because we regard it as a commodity belonging to us. When we see land as a community to which we belong, we may begin to use it with love and respect."
—Aldo Leopold

Conclusion

THE LAND STEWARDSHIP CONCEPTS that defined the first conservation movement in the United States in the late nineteenth century—scientific management, sustained yield, and the protection of the long-term productivity of soil and water resources—have served this nation well for a hundred years. In response to changes in the global environment and in social values and attitudes toward the land and natural resources, the demands placed upon resource managers as land stewards have grown. Building upon the solid foundation of a century of conservation, the concepts of land stewardship are growing and changing to fulfill these expanding needs.

The group of individuals gathered at Grey Towers to explore these expanding needs, and the role of resource managers in meeting them, defined land stewardship by distilling their many ideas down to four key principles:

1. Management activities must be within the physical and biological capabilities of the land, based upon comprehensive, up-to-date resource information and a thorough scientific understanding of the ecosystem's functioning and response.

2. The intent of management, as well as monitoring and reporting, should be making progress toward desired future resource conditions, not on achieving specific near-term resource output targets.

3. Stewardship means passing the land and resources—including intact, functioning forest ecosystems—to the next generation in better condition than they were found.

4.   Land stewardship must be more than good "scientific management"; it must be a moral imperative.

Social needs and values will continue to evolve, just as they have in the past. The concepts of what constitutes good land stewardship will also continue to evolve, and society will look to its resource managers for leadership as the definition of conservation continues to expand to meet the needs of a changing world. To be truly responsive, however, resource managers must remember to talk to more than just one another. It will be increasingly important that people other than resource management professionals—people with different per-spectives that may not always be consistent with those of resource managers—be explicitly brought into the process and listened to.

The next step after defining good land stewardship is to demonstrate its application on the land. Resource managers will learn best by example, and this will give professionals and non-professionals alike an opportunity to recognize good land stewardship when they see it. The principles outlined above, the "Grey Towers Protocol" as they have been called, should become a set of core values to be learned, reinforced, and incorporated into the internal value system of every resource management professional. This light, once lit, should not be hid under a bushel. As important as these principles might be in guiding the physical activities of resource managers on the land, they may be even more valuable as a means for resource managers to communicate a vision of steward-ship and personal responsibility to society at large, helping a fragmented public to recognize that our economic well-being, as well as our environmental health, rests on our being able to pull together rather than pull apart.

The Creative Act of 1891 represented a revolution in this nation's philoso-phy and attitude toward its land and natural resources. It marked the end of one era and the beginning of another, the first great era of conservation. One hundred years later we recognize more clearly just how important that transi-tion was to later generations of Americans, including our own. We are privileged to live at a time when the nation is poised to enter the next great era of conservation and to have some role in defining and leading that effort. We can only hope that the generation a century from now will credit us with the same courage, foresight, and strength of conviction that we now commemo-rate in the conservation leaders of a century ago.

"*When the best leader's work is done, the people say, 'We did it ourselves.'*"

—Lao-tzu

Literature Cited

[1] Marsh, George Perkins, *Man and Nature; or, Physical Geography as Modified by Human Action* (New York: 1864).

[2] *Ibid.* See also: Perlin, John, *A Forest Journey* (New York: Norton, 1989).

[3] Genesis 1: 27-28 as translated in *The Holy Bible*, Revised Standard Edition (New York: Thomas Nelson and Sons, 1953).

[4] Genesis 2:15.

[5] For a detailed historical discussion of the influence of Christian philosophy on environmental awareness, see: Nash, Roderick, *The Rights of Nature: A History of Environmental Ethics* (Madison, WI: University of Wisconsin Press, 1989), pp. 87-120.

[6] Nash, Roderick, *Wilderness and the American Mind*, Third Edition (New Haven, CT: Yale University Press, 1982), p. 105.

[7] Clepper, Henry, *The Crusade for Conservation* (Washington, DC: The American Forestry Association, 1975).

[8] *Ibid.*

[9] "Report of the Commissioner of Agriculture" (Washington, DC: U.S. Department of Agriculture, 1865), p. 219.

[10]"Annual Report of the Secretary of the Interior for the Year Ending June 30, 1869" (Washington, DC: Department of the Interior, 1869).

[11]"Creative Act of March 3, 1891," Ch. 561, 26 Stat. 1095, 1103, repealed by 90 Stat. 2792 (1976).

[12]Dana, Samuel T. and Fairfax, Sally K., *Forest and Range Policy: Its Development in the United States* (New York: McGraw-Hill, 1980), pp. 29, 56-58.

[13]"Organic Administration Act of 1897," Ch. 2, 30 Stat. 11, as amended; 16 U.S.C. 473-475, 477-482, 551.

[14]Dana and Fairfax, *Forest and Range Policy*, p. 58.

[15]"Act of March 1, 1911," Ch. 186, 36 Stat. 961, as amended; 16 U.S.C. 480.

[16]National Research Council, *Forestry Research: A Mandate for Change* (Washington, DC: National Academy Press, 1990).

[17]Daellenbach, H.G. and George, J. A., *Introduction to Operations Research Techniques* (Boston: Allyn and Bacon, Inc., 1978), pp. 26, 74-80.

[18]Leopold, Aldo, *A Sand County Almanac, and Sketches Here and There* (New York: Oxford University Press, 1949), p. 210.

[19]*Ibid.,* p. 214.

[20]Gup, Ted, "Down With the God Squad," *Time,* November 5, 1990.

[21]See generally: Nash, *The Rights of Nature.*

[22]Leopold, *A Sand County Almanac,* pp. 201-202.

[23]Nash, *The Rights of Nature,* pp. 6-9.

[24]Leopold, *A Sand County Almanac,* pp. 224-225. The first statement of these ideas occurred in "The Conservation Ethic," *Journal of Forestry,* 31 (1933), 634-643.

[25]Franklin, W., *Paper Recycling: The View to 1995* (New York: American Paper Institute, 1990).

[26]Kanter, Rosabeth M., *When Giants Learn to Dance* (New York: Simon and Schuster, 1990). See also: Kanter, R.M., *The Change Masters: Innovation for Productivity in the American Corporation* (New York: Touchstone Books, 1985).

"The insufferable arrogance of human beings to think that Nature was made solely for their benefit, as if it was conceivable that the sun had been set afire merely to ripen men's apples and head their cabbages."

—Cyrano de Bergerac

Bibliography

THIS BIBLIOGRAPHY IS PROVIDED FOR READERS who may wish to learn more about the evolution of land stewardship concepts and environmental ethics. The authors explore these ideas from both philosophical and religious perspectives, showing that the origins of the concepts are hardly new but have been a part of the cultures of many different societies for centuries or even millennia. The list is not meant to be comprehensive but to provide a doorway into several different areas of literature that readers may wish to explore.*

Anglemyer, Mary, Seagraves, Eleanor, and LeMaistre, Catherine, *A Search for Environmental Ethics: An Initial Bibliography* (Washington, DC: Smithsonian Institution Press, 1980).

Attfield, Robin, *The Ethics of Environmental Concern* (New York: Columbia University Press, 1983).

Barbour, Ian G. (ed.), *Earth Might Be Fair: Reflections on Ethics, Religion and Ecology* (Englewood Cliffs, NJ: Prentice-Hall, 1972).

Barbour, Ian G. (ed.), *Western Man and Environmental Ethics: Attitudes*

---

* The author wishes to thank James A. Nash, Executive Director of the Center for Theology and Public Policy in Washington, DC, and Sara Ebenreck, Editor of the monthly *Earth Ethics* published in Prince Frederick, Maryland, for their assistance in developing this bibliography.

Toward Nature and Technology (Reading, MA: Addison-Wesley, 1983).

Berry, Thomas, *A Dream of the Earth* (San Francisco: Sierra Club Books, 1988).

Berry, Wendell, *Home Economics* (San Francisco: North Point Press, 1987).

Bowman, Douglas, *Beyond the Modern Mind: The Spiritual and Ethical Challenge of the Environmental Crisis* (New York: Pilgrim Press, 1990).

Cahn, Robert, *Footprints on the Planet: A Search for an Environmental Ethic* (New York: University Books, 1978).

Carmody, John, *Ecology and Religion: Toward a New Christian Theology of Nature* (New York: Paulist Press, 1983).

Commoner, Barry, *The Closing Circle: Nature, Man and Technology* (New York: Alfred A. Knopf, 1971).

Daly, Herman E. and Cobb, John B. Jr., *For the Common Good: Redirecting the Economy Toward Community, the Environment, and a Sustainable Future* (Boston: Beacon Press, 1989).

Diamond, Irene and Orenstein, Gloria Feman, *Reweaving the World: The Emergence of Ecofeminism* (San Francisco: Sierra Club Books, 1990).

Dubos, Rene, *The Wooing of the Earth: New Perspectives on Man's Use of Nature* (New York: Scribner's, 1980).

Eisley, Loren, *The Immense Journey* (New York: Vintage, 1971).

Emerson, Ralph Waldo, *Nature Addresses and Lectures* (Boston: Houghton Mifflin Co., 1903).

Frankel, Charles, "The Rights of Nature," in Tribe, Laurence H., Schnelling, Corrine S., and Vos, John (eds), *When Values Conflict* (Cambridge, MA: Ballinger [Lippincott], 1976).

Glacken, Clarence J., *Traces on the Rhodian Shore: Nature and Culture in Western Thought from Ancient Times to the End of the Eighteenth Century* (Berkeley: University of California Press, 1967).

Granberg-Michaelson, Wesley (ed.), *Tending the Garden: Essays on the Gospel and the Earth* (Grand Rapids, MI: Eerdmans, 1987).

Gray, Elizabeth Dodson, *Green Paradise Lost* (Wellesley, MA: Roundtable Press, 1981).

Hall, Douglas J., *Imaging God: Dominion as Stewardship* (Grand Rapids, MI: Eerdmans, 1986).

Ihde, Don, *Technology and the Lifeworld: From Garden to Earth* (Bloomington: Indiana University Press).

Johnson, Lawrence E., *A Morally Deep World: An Essay on Moral Significance and Environmental Ethics* (New York: Cambridge University Press, 1990).

Leopold, Aldo, *A Sand County Almanac, and Sketches Here and There* (New York: Oxford University Press, 1949).

Lilburne, Geoffrey R., *A Sense of Place: A Christian Theology of the Land* (Nashville, TN: Abingdon, 1989).

McCormick, John, *Reclaiming Paradise: The Global Environmental Movement* (Bloomington, IN: Indiana University Press, 1989).

McLuhan, T.C., *Touch the Earth: A Self-Portrait of Indian Existence* (New York: Promontory Press, 1971).

Mills, Stephanie (ed.), *In Praise of Nature* (Covelo, CA: Island Press, 1990).

Moule, C.F.D., *Man and Nature in the New Testament: Some Reflections on Biblical Ecology* (Philadelphia: Fortress Press, 1967).

Murphy, Charles M., *At Home On Earth: Foundations for a Catholic Ethic of the Environment* (New York: Crossroad, 1989).

Nash, Roderick (ed.), *American Environmentalism: Readings in Conservation History* (New York: McGraw-Hill, 1990).

Nash, Roderick F., *The Rights of Nature: A History of Environmental Ethics* (Madison: University of Wisconsin Press, 1989).

Nash, Roderick F., *Wilderness and the American Mind* (New Haven: Yale University Press, 1967).

Norton, Bryan C., *The Preservation of Species* (Princeton: Princeton University Press, 1986).

Novak, Barbara, *Nature and Culture: American Landscape and Painting, 1825-1875.* (New York: Oxford University Press, 1980).

Passmore, John, *Man's Responsibility for Nature: Ecological Problems and Western Tradition* (London: Duckworth, 1980).

Perlin, John, *A Forest Journey: The Role of Wood in the Development of Civilization* (New York: W.W. Norton, 1989).

Perlin, John, *The Expendable Future: U.S. Politics and the Protection of Biological Diversity* (Durham: Duke University Press, 1990).

Piaseki, Bruce and Asmus, Peter, *In Search of Environmental Excellence: Moving Beyond Blame* (New York: Simon and Schuster, 1990).

Rolston, Holmes III, *Environmental Ethics: Duties to and Values in the Natural World* (Philadelphia: Temple University Press, 1988).

Rolston, Holmes III, *Philosophy Gone Wild* (Buffalo: Prometheus Books, 1986).

Santmire, H. Paul, *The Travail of Nature: The Ambiguous Ecological Promise of Christian Theology* (Philadelphia: Fortress Press, 1985).

Sikora, Robert I. and Barry, Brian (eds.), *Obligations to Future Generations* (Philadelphia: Temple University Press, 1978).

Snyder, Gary, *The Practice of the Wild* (San Francisco: North Point Press, 1990).

Stout, Benjamin B. (ed.), *Forests in the Here and Now: A Collection of the Writings of Hugh Miller Raup.* (Missoula, MT: Montana Forest and Conservation Experiment Station, 1981).

Swierenga, Robert P. (ed.), *James C. Malin: History and Ecology: Studies of the Grassland* (Lincoln: University of Nebraska Press, 1984).

Taylor, Paul W., *Respect for Nature: A Theory of Environmental Ethics* (Princeton: Princeton University Press, 1986).

Thomas, Keith, *Man and the Natural World: A History of the Modern Sensibility* (New York: Pantheon, 1983).

Udall, Stewart, *The Quiet Crisis,* Second Edition (New York: Henry Holt, 1988).

Wallace-Hadrill, David S., *The Greek Patristic View of Nature* (New York: Barnes and Noble, 1968).

Wilson, Edward O., *Biophilia: The Human Bond With Other Species* (Cambridge: Harvard University Press, 1984).

Wilson, Edward O. (ed.), *Biodiversity* (Washington, DC: National Academy Press, 1988).

World Commission on Environment and Development, *Our Common Future* ("The Brundtland Commission Report") (New York: Oxford University Press, 1987). For a summary of this report see: Lebel, Gregory and Kane, Hal, *Sustainable Development: A Guide to Our Common Future* (Washington, DC: Global Tomorrow Coalition, 1989).

Young, John, *Sustaining the Earth* (Cambridge: Harvard University Press, 1990).

GREY TOWERS